ELTHAM
IN OLD PHOTOGRAPHS

THIS IS AVERY HILL ROAD when it was a country lane known as Southwood Road. It was widened in 1930. The junctions of Cradley Road and Sidewood Road would now be seen in the area to the right of this picture. In earlier times this lane was also known as Pope Street – a name given to part of a larger area now called New Eltham.

ELTHAM
IN OLD PHOTOGRAPHS

—————COLLECTED BY—————
JOHN KENNETT

ALAN SUTTON

Alan Sutton Publishing
Phoenix Mill · Far Thrupp · Stroud · Gloucestershire

First published 1991

British Library Cataloguing in Publication Data

Eltham in old photographs.
I. Kennett, John, *1939–*
942.162

ISBN 0-86299-965-0

Front Cover Illustration:
THE VIEW OF THE GREYHOUND AND MELLINS in Eltham High Street is almost unchanged today although the horse and cart and Thomas Tillings have long gone.

Typeset in 9/10 Korinna.
Typesetting and origination by
Alan Sutton Publishing Limited.
Printed in Great Britain by
The Bath Press, Avon.

CONTENTS

This book is dedicated
to my wife Marion

AN EIGHTEENTH-CENTURY ARTIST'S VIEW of the buildings of Eltham Palace.

INTRODUCTION

Eltham is a community whose age is undateable, but evidence of Roman and Saxon occupation has been discovered. By the time of the Norman Conquest, Eltham was an established community and accordingly found a place in the Domesday Book of 1086. Eltham Palace was created in medieval times from Bishop Bek's residence and from lands particularly at Middle Park and Horn Park, which were enclosed for Royal use when the Court was at Eltham. Although Henry VIII 'was much at Eltham', he preferred his palace at Greenwich which was easily reached by boat from Westminster, compared with the overland route to Eltham. The palace fell out of Royal favour after the Tudors, and became ruinous particularly as a result of the Civil War. Many of the trees from the Royal Parks were felled, and used for ship building at the dockyards on the River Thames. With the Royal deer slaughtered and the woods denuded, the Crown lands were taken over for farming which brought a change in land use to the southern parts of Eltham.

Eltham was a Kentish village with its main inhabitants living near the area of the High Street and St John's church, the known history of which dates to 1160. To the north of the village lay a collection of Tudor buildings at the centre of the Well Hall estate, which was held by the Roper family until 1733. William Roper's initials can still be seen on brickwork at a corner of the surviving Tudor Barn.

The rural scene gradually changed with the coming of the Dartford Loop Railway in 1866 when a station named Eltham (known today as Mottingham) was established. House building took place principally at Mottingham Village, Court Road, and around the eastern end of North Park. Pope Street (New Eltham) developed after 1878, when the railway station opened, with houses, public house, churches and shops.

Major developments followed the opening of the Bexleyheath Railway of 1895 in the form of the Corbett Estate at Well Hall and Eltham Park. The railways brought better communications with London, while a tram link was established with Woolwich in 1910. The change from rural to suburban Eltham was captured photographically by the picture postcard companies who were keen to exploit this popular hobby. Many pre-First World War postcards were produced of Eltham which give us a view of a community which had a narrow winding High Street and where the horse was the main source of power on farms and highways. Views from this era are produced in this book together with later pictures, which show the transition from the village days through people, transport and buildings, which all make up some of the Eltham patchwork.

Change is often not welcomed especially when an existing pattern of life is threatened through the removal of a well-loved building or institution. The ravages of aerial bombardment during the Second World War were quite profound and affected not only the fabric of the town but people's lives. Some of Eltham's open spaces were sacrificed for the construction of Sidcup Road which was known as the Eltham bypass when completed in 1923. The effect of the development of a new London traffic artery through Eltham can be seen with the recent completion of the Rochester Way Relief Road which involved further demolition.

These pictures reveal a way of life gone for ever, best recalled through photographs. I am aware that it is impossible to cover all aspects of Eltham, but I hope that readers will enjoy my selection of pictures.

King Henry VI Act I scene i

Exeter   To Eltham will I, where the young king is,
                    Being ordain'd his special governor;
                    And for his safety there I'll best devise.

Winchester   Each hath his place and function to attend:
                    I am left out; for me nothing remains.
                    But long I will not be Jack-out-of-office:
                    The king from Eltham I intend to steal
                    And sit at chiefest stern of public weal.

                                        William Shakespeare

Rural Aspects and Farming

AN ELTHAM PHOTOGRAPHER stands poised at the entrance to Gravel Pit Lane. He, with many others, recorded the people, places, and happenings of Eltham and a selection of their work is recorded here as a tribute to the art of the photographer.

ELTHAM HILL with Lyme Farm on the left.

THESE HEALTHY HAYSTACKS were created near the farmhouse and buildings of Lyme Farm, Eltham Hill, which stood on the site now occupied by the Eltham Hill Working Men's Club and nearby houses. The farmer Mr W. Corp is at the top of the ladder, his son Gordon is in the white coat.

MR AND MRS W. CORP of Lyme Farm ready to take a spin.

WORKERS AT LYME FARM take a rest from mucking out the animal sheds.

THE NAME 'NELL GWYNN'S COTTAGES' was created by the postcard publishers. These cottages have no known connection with the famous lady, although she would have probably been familiar with the style of building. The Shell petrol station in Well Hall Road now occupies this site.

THE ELTHAM DAIRY was established in 1866 with a High Street shop on the site of the present Halfords. At this time it was run by Mr J. Howe, with milk being supplied from Belmont Park Farm at Green Lane, New Eltham. Note the large churns of milk on the carts.

THE MEADOWS to the rear of Holy Trinity church and Vicarage, Southend Crescent.

PIPPENHALL FARM, BEXLEY ROAD, when Mr J. Grace was the farmer. Pippenhall Farm Stables now occupy the site of the former farmhouse.

ON A FIELD ADJOINING THIS RURAL CHAPEL FARM SCENE a cricket pitch was created by the Eltham Cricket Club where Dr W. G. Grace played as a member.

MR PALMER WITH HIS SHIRE HORSES ploughing a field at Coldharbour Farm where Ruxley Manor School now stands.

HORSEPOWER in use at Clay Farm, New Eltham.

THIS WATER TROUGH for horses was a welcome stop at Clare Corner. Removed in 1966, it was discovered in a Greenwich council yard, and put back on the green for its new use as a plant trough in 1987.

THIS PICTURE was painted in 1867 when the present Southwood Road was known as Cross Lane. An Edwardian view of the same location on p. 17 shows the effect of housing development following the construction of the Dartford Loop Railway.

NOS 1 AND 2 SOUTHWOOD ROAD WEST, almost opposite Bercta Road. The cottages were removed for road widening in 1930 and the land behind is now the Southwood Road Recreation Ground.

SPARROWS LANE when it really was a lane.

HORN PARK FARM. William Walter Wood was the farmer earlier this century but he also traded as a florist, fruiterer and greengrocer with shops at Lee, Eltham and Blackheath.

THE FORMER MIDDLE PARK FARMHOUSE was demolished in 1973 to make way for the flats of Blann Close which were named after local councillor Mr T. Blann.

THE LATE MR. W. BLENKIRON.

MR WILLIAM BLENKIRON was a successful shirtmaker in Wood Street, London and lived at Dalston where he kept horses in a back garden stable. In 1852 he moved to Eltham where he leased Middle Park Farm from the Crown and established his Middle Park Stud Farm which received international acclaim. He bred Derby winners including Hermit who won the 1867 race in a snowstorm. In 1866 he established the annual Middle Park Stakes at Newmarket which is usually run at the end of September. He died in 1871 and was buried at St John's churchyard where his tall family tomb can be seen near that of Colonel North of Avery Hill.

EIGHTEENTH-CENTURY PRINTS OF ELTHAM PALACE show cattle in and around the ancient buildings. This tradition was carried on until 1988 when Mr Stanley Mitchell gave up the lease on King John's Walk Farm which had been previously held by his father Mr Wilfred Mitchell. The top picture shows cattle in a field by King John's Walk while the recently demolished farm buildings are featured in the lower view.

THIS MUST BE A FAMILY VISIT to the hop fields at New Eltham as they do not look prepared for hop picking themselves. The fields were used as the site for the houses in the Old Farm Avenue area.

WORKING HORSES are rarely seen in action today except possibly pulling rag and bone carts. Well-known 'totter' Mr W. Johnson plies his trade in Larchwood Road with his horse who is not averse to taking food from sympathetic residents or their children.

TAKEN IN EARLY 1915 this picture shows work starting on the housing development now known as the Progress Estate. The photographer is standing in front of the gardens of the houses at Craigton Road. 'Nell Gwynn's Cottages' (see p. 12) can be seen to the left. The tram poles are just discernible alongside Well Hall Road which crosses this rural view.

PARTS OF CROWN WOODS LANE SURVIVE TODAY among the woods of Shooters Hill but this section was transformed for the Eltham Heights Estate. See the picture on p. 58 for a contrasting scene.

SECTION TWO

Buildings Historical

The Banquet Hall. King John's Palace. Eltham

AN EDWARDIAN VIEW of the south side of the Great Hall at Eltham Palace shows some crumbling masonry and open windows. The name 'King John's Palace' is misleading in that the association is with King John of France who was a prisoner here in 1356 and not King John of England.

A PRINT of 1832 showing the medieval bridge at Eltham Palace.

MOAT HOUSE and the bridge at Eltham Palace.

THE LACK OF WINDOWS makes Eltham Palace's Great Hall look draughty and uncared for in this Edwardian view. Major improvements were completed by the Office of Works in 1914 when the roof was greatly strengthened by steel bracing.

THE GREAT HALL AND MOAT from the east. This view was greatly altered when Mr S. Courtauld built Eltham Hall in the 1930s which necessitated the removal of the Victorian Moat House to the right.

THE GREAT HALL (c. 1479) as restored for Stephen Courtauld in 1936.

THE TUDOR BUILDING of the Lord Chancellor's Lodgings was the residence for Cardinal Wolsey when he came to stay at Eltham Palace. Restoration in 1952 gave back the Tudor look to the properties which are here covered by weatherboarding.

THE EFFIGY AND TOMB OF PRINCE JOHN OF ELTHAM at Westminster Abbey. He was born at Eltham Palace in 1316 and since September 1966 children from Eltham primary schools have taken roses from his birthplace to lay on his tomb. This annual commemoration, which takes place in September, is sponsored by The Eltham Society.

ELTHAM LODGE was built in 1664 for Sir John Shaw who was granted the lease to the Manor of Eltham on the Restoration of the Monarchy after the Civil War. The Shaw family retained the Crown lease until it was transferred to Mr Benjamin Wood in 1838. In 1892 the house and grounds were taken over by the Eltham Golf Club who amalgamated with The Royal Blackheath Golf Club in 1923.

WELL HALL HOUSE was built after 1733 by Sir Gregory Page of Wricklemarsh House, Blackheath, who had acquired the Roper Estate at Well Hall. It was used as a home and workshop by clock and watchmaker John Arnold around 1790 and in 1899 became the home of Mr Bland and his wife, the children's author Edith Nesbit. The house stood opposite the Royal Arsenal Co-operative Society (RACS) store and was demolished as part of the scheme to create Well Hall Pleasaunce.

THE TUDOR BARN AT WELL HALL PLEASAUNCE was opened in 1936 after extensive restoration had transformed it from a farm building into an art gallery and restaurant.

SIR WILLIAM JAMES worked for the East India Company. During his adventurous life he drove pirates off the island fortress at Severndroog on the Malabar coast of India. Following his death Lady James had Severndroog Castle (lower picture) erected in 1784 on the slopes of Shooters Hill as a memorial to her husband. The top picture shows their home at Park Farm Place (now the site of St Mary's School in Glenure Road) with Severndroog Castle in the distance.

THE SPIRE OF THE OLD ST JOHN'S CHURCH became part of the rebuilt church of 1875, but by 1880 had been replaced by the present spire which has become a distinctive local landmark (see opposite page). The original footpath still goes through the churchyard and is bounded by the old brick wall which contains some flint work. Note the old roadside water pump. The first recorded vicar was Adam de Bromleigh in 1160.

THIS 1930S PICTURE SHOWS ST JOHN'S CHURCH AND HITCHES GARAGE on the left which was established in 1897 before cars became popular. Together with the Paint and Varnish Works next door it suffered extensive damage from a V1 rocket attack in 1944, and the showroom had to be rebuilt.

THIS EIGHTEENTH-CENTURY ICE WELL was discovered on the site of classroom extensions at the Ave Maria School (now St Mary's School), Glenure Road, and had to be filled in before work could commence. A similar structure can be seen at the Tarn public park in Court Road.

THE ROAD FROM LEE TO FOOTSCRAY THROUGH ELTHAM AND NEW ELTHAM was administered by the New Cross Turnpike Trust from 1781 until 1865. Fees from travellers were collected at their Lee toll-house. Milestones were set up along the roadside and several still survive like this one in Footscray Road by Southend House (opposite the B&Q store).

AT AVERY HILL, Colonel North the 'Nitrate King' had by 1890, created an elegant country house with grounds stretching from New Eltham to Shooters Hill. The London County Council bought the house and immediate grounds in 1902 using the mansion from 1904 as a training college for lady teachers while the grounds were laid out as Avery Hill Park.

COLONEL NORTH'S FORMER MANSION can be seen in this 1920s aerial picture of Avery Hill College. Most of the east wing was demolished in the Second World War and subsequently rebuilt to a different style.

THE VICTORIAN MOTTINGHAM HOUSE in Mottingham Lane stood on the site of Mottingham Place which was built in 1560. The flats of Colview Court are here today.

MOTTINGHAM HIGH ROAD at Mottingham village with some still recognizable buildings, although the first two on the right have been replaced by shops of the mid-1930s.

THE ORIGINAL GEFFRYE ALMSHOUSES at Kingsland Road, London E2 were established with funds bequeathed by Sir Robert Geffrye in 1714 and are now used as the Geffrye Museum. The new almshouses, with a statue of the founder, were built by the Worshipful Company of Ironmongers in 1912 at Mottingham, but are now in private residential use.

THIS BUILDING was erected in 1883 as three almshouses for the Thomas Philipot Charity with gardens to the front. It was sold and altered by Eltham builder Mr W. Childs as temporary accommodation for Barclays Bank when their premises were being rebuilt. From 1933 it was used principally for the Halifax Building Society and was replaced in 1974 with their new offices.

THE SIX ORIGINAL PHILIPOT ALMSHOUSES of 1694 were financed from Thomas Philipot's legacy and housed four Eltham and two Chislehurst residents. The building stood in the High Street to the west of Blunts Road, until it was demolished in 1929. One of the horse-box doors is preserved in the Greenwich Museum at Plumstead Library. The original 1694 date stone has been incorporated into the replacement almshouses at Philipot Path.

THE ELTHAM WORKHOUSE was opened in 1738 at a cost of £313. In this century the property was used as almshouses until demolished in 1964. The replacement Fifteenpenny Field Almshouses in Blunts Road were opened in 1963.

PARK PLACE WAS RENAMED PASSEY PLACE in 1938. The chapel was originally built for the Bible Christians in 1880 but was demolished in 1972 with other property for an extension to the Caters supermarket. The Park Tavern stands on the right of the picture.

HOLY TRINITY CHURCH opened in 1869 to serve a new residential area. The Revd Henry A. Hall was vicar from 1907 to 1942 and during the Gallipoli campaign of 1915 he was Chaplain to the 29th Division. In 1917 a Gallipoli Memorial Chapel was established in the church and an annual commemoration is still held, now under the auspices of the Gallipoli Memorial Trust.

ST SAVIOUR'S CHURCH at Middle Park Avenue was opened in 1933 to serve the new estate which had not been built here when this photograph was taken.

ST SAVIOUR'S CHURCH AT MIDDLE PARK was designed by the architects Welch, Cachemaille-Day, and Lander and is of particular interest to devotees of 1930s architecture.

THIS CHURCH WAS DESIGNED BY SIR GILBERT SCOTT and from 1857 stood in Woolwich Dockyard. It was taken down and re-erected as the permanent church for St Barnabas at Well Hall and consecrated in 1933. Serious damage was caused by an enemy air raid in 1944 and restoration was not completed until 1957. Former Eltham resident and St Barnabas' church member, comedian Frankie Howerd, renamed the church hall in his favour in 1988. The hutment to the left of the church was replaced by the vicarage.

ELTHAM LIBRARY opened in 1906 as part of an abortive civic development which was to incude a town hall and swimming baths. Demolition of old cottages, Metcalfe's forge and the relocation of The Rising Sun was all part of this scheme by Woolwich Borough Council. 'Sun Yard' is perpetuated in the name of the council yard in Archery Road on part of the old public house site.

THIS GRACEFUL GEORGIAN HOUSE with gardens to front and rear was taken over by the South Metropolitan Gas Company from 1916. On its site the gas showrooms and a Marks and Spencer Store (now Debenhams) were built, both opening in 1938.

THE ORANGERY stood at the end of the garden of Eltham House. This view from 1964 shows parked vans from nearby Bon Ton Laundry in front of the Orangery when few people knew of the existence of this Grade II listed building recorded by the Department of the Environment. Many plans have been made for its restoration, but no work has ever taken place and fire, vandalism and weathering have reduced the building to a shell. Ownership is with Greenwich Council.

CLIEFDEN HOUSE in 1929 not long after it lost its front garden for road widening which necessitated the creation of the high pavement which is still in use today. The former Cliefden stables stand behind the old house and both properties are Grade II listed. In the 1920s the Bon Ton Laundry was built on the rear garden.

A MOTORIZED FIRE-APPLIANCE stands ready for action in the forecourt at Eltham Fire Station which opened in 1904. Note the narrowness of the High Street.

ELTHAM AND MOTTINGHAM COTTAGE HOSPITAL was relocated to its present site in Passey Place in 1898 from a house just west of St John's church. The footpath was then known as Back Lane and was renamed Philipot Path in 1937 due to its proximity to the relocated Philipot Almshouses (1931).

BARN HOUSE at Bexley Road was demolished together with Conduit Lodge to facilitate the building of the Pippenhall Estate by Woolwich Borough Council in 1961. There was local resentment about the loss of these two historic buildings.

THE WIDENING OF FOOTSCRAY ROAD in 1923 included a new wall for Graftons factory while the old garden wall of Southend House on the opposite side of the road remained intact.

WITH THE ADDITION OF A CONSERVATORY AND A LARGE GARDEN, this Victorian farmhouse was converted to an Edwardian country residence, Southend Hall, for Mr A.C. Latter and his family. It was acquired by the War Office in 1937 and housed the Air Defence 338th Anti-Aircraft Company RE (TA) for which the drill hall on the right was added. The housing development of Inca Drive now covers this area.

THE BUILDINGS BEHIND THE ROAD ROLLER have been replaced by the Eltham Pools (1939), while The White Hart to the left of the workmen was superseded by the present public house in 1926. The former hostelry is featured in Jeffery Farnol's novel *The Amateur Gentleman* which was published in 1913.

THE ELTHAM BREWERY nestles behind the trees of the garden of St John's church Vicarage on the left, while almost opposite among the shops stands the former Chequers public house, with an old milestone on the pavement.

THE KINGS ARMS in an uncrowded High Street scene opposite St John's church. The pub and adjacent shops were demolished when the road was widened for a tram route extension.

COURT YARD WITH THE OLD ELM TREE which was blown down in 1903, near The Crown. By the Congregational church stands a house which was demolished when Well Hall Road was put through in 1905 from the Well Hall railway bridge.

THE CASTLE HOTEL had been newly built when this picture was taken and included a pleasure garden and a yard for horses.

THE CARPENTERS ARMS was built at the turn of the century and replaced an older hostelry. This view from 1964 includes the Caters grocery shop whose business was transferred to a new supermarket at Passey Place in 1968. The Carpenters Arms was demolished in 1986 and Next has taken the new shop.

THE BEEHIVE was rebuilt in 1897 and incorporated a pleasure ground at the rear of the public house where travelling fairs were sometimes staged. Brentwood Close has now been built on this land. The houses opposite The Beehive were known as Pelham Terrace.

THE SEVENTEENTH-CENTURY COTTAGES at Pound Place survived to the 1920s as did the sweet shop which was popular with children from the Eltham National Schools.

SECTION THREE

Housing

THIS DIMINUTIVE PROPERTY known as Rose Cottage stood near the present junction of Sherard Road and Lassa Road.

RED-CROFT, ELTHAM.

RED-CROFT stood at the junction of Court Road and Court Yard and was the home, until 1924, of Mrs J. North, widow of Colonel North of Avery Hill. Together with another large house it was demolished for the 1960 development of Moat Court.

THE ENTRANCE TO JUBILEE COTTAGES off the High Street was known as Outtrim's Yard due to the family business which was located here. In this picture the former Eltham Brewery on the left is used as the Eltham Baptist Meeting Room. Note the one-legged girl and the children nearby who could have given inspiration to E. Nesbit for her book *The Railway Children* which was written at Well Hall. The side entrance to Allders store is here today.

SOUTHWOOD COTTAGES with the road passing close to the garden fences. When Avery Hill Road was widened and straightened in 1930 a green was created in front of the cottages. In 1922 Southwood Road East was renamed Avery Hill Road.

THE LAND FOR SALE is now the site of New Eltham Library with Southwood Road passing the cottage shown on pp. 16 and 17. The stable to the rear of the doctor's house on the left is used by the 18th Royal Eltham Scout Group as their headquarters. Note the Victorian pillar box and the fire alarm.

THE ELEGANT HOUSE AND GROUNDS OF KINGS GARDEN was replaced by the houses of Kings Orchard from the mid-1930s.

WOODFORD LODGE STOOD AT THE SOUTHERN END OF VICTORIA ROAD (now Footscray Road) and was demolished for road-widening in 1965 which did not take place. It was once known as Stepstile House when the path alongside was Love Lane.

MANY SCOTTISH PLACES are recorded in the road names of Cameron Corbett's estate at Well Hall and Eltham Park which he developed between 1900 and 1914, when war stopped building operations. All houses were sold on 999 year leases and ranged from terraced to detached houses. The developer was a Glasgow MP from 1885 to 1911, when he was created Lord Rowallan. This title was inherited by his son who also became Chief Scout from 1945 to 1959.

THE FIRST PAGE ESTATE comprising houses at Sherard Road, Spencer Gardens, Lassa Road and Everest Road was built by W.C. Brake after the completion of the Well Hall Road between Well Hall and the High Street in 1905. Sherard Road shown here was the original thoroughfare between Well Hall and Eltham. The houses on the left were rebuilt after a V1 rocket attack in 1944. The former nursery land opposite became the site of the Well Hall bus station from 1952 to 1985.

THE GOVERNMENT built an estate for Woolwich Arsenal munition workers and their families at Well Hall in 1915. In 1925 it was sold to the RACS and named the Progress Estate. This early view of the estate is at Moira Road, but today the policeman would probably be knocked over if he stood in this position as the Rochester Way now cuts across the scene. The Progress Estate is now a Conservation Area.

IN THE ELTHAM PARK AND WELL HALL AREA 1,500 wooden hutments were erected for Woolwich Arsenal munition workers in 1916, with the largest concentration being on the unbuilt Corbett Estate. Many and varied businesses were allowed to operate, including a grocery shop, from the front room of this hut. The author's volume *The Eltham Hutments* gives fuller details of this unique housing development which has been replaced by permanent housing.

HOSTELS FOR SINGLE PEOPLE who worked on First World War munition production at Woolwich Arsenal were erected here at Well Hall Road and through to Archery Road. They were removed in the early 1920s.

A PASSENGER LEAVES THE 44 TRAM on Eltham Hill by the Page Estate which was the first major housing development undertaken by the Woolwich Borough Council on the agricultural land of Lyme Farm. The estate took ten years to complete. Compare this scene with an earlier view on p. 10.

SOME OF THE FIRST HOUSES of Charles and Daniel Barwell's Belmont Estate can be seen here at Larchwood Road. They were fitted with wooden window frames, but later properties like those at Sidcup Road, Montbelle Road, Felhampton Road and Charldane Road had metal frames which were produced at the Crittalls factory on the Sidcup bypass. 'Charldane' is an amalgam of the first names of the developers.

MIDDLE PARK FARM was bought from the Crown by Woolwich Borough Council and a new housing estate was commenced in 1931 principally to rehouse the residents of the Eltham hutments. The telephone box has recently been restored as it is Grade II listed and stands at the junction of Eltham Palace Road and The Vista.

THE CROWN LEASED LAND FOR HOUSING to Eltham builder Mr J. Webb for his Eltham Heights Estate which was started in 1934 here at Crown Woods Way, which was transformed from the rural Crown Woods Lane as seen on p. 22.

THE HUTMENTS AT ELTHAM PARK were replaced with permanent houses from 1935 by Percy Bilton Ltd as shown here at Glenesk Road.

DETAILS OF NEW HOUSES on the Sidcup Road from the mid-1930s.

THE DAVIS ESTATE, DOMONIC DRIVE,
NEW ELTHAM, S.E.9.

Type S.F.2. Two Reception Rooms - Three Bedrooms.

NO ROAD
CHARGES,
LEGAL
COSTS OR
SURVEY FEES.

INTERIOR
DECORATIONS
TO
PURCHASER'S
CHOICE

SEMI-DETACHED.

£730 From 17/1 Weekly.

Crown Lease: Ground Rent £7.10.0 per annum.

DETACHED: **£805** Leasehold, from **18/10** Weekly. G.R. £8.10.0 per annum.

ACCOMMODATION.

DRAWING ROOM — 13' 1" x 12' 4".	FIRST BEDROOM — 13' 1" x 11' 5".	
DINING ROOM — 12' 6" x 11' 1".	SECOND BEDROOM — 12' 6" x 11' 5".	
	THIRD BEDROOM — 9' 1" x 6' 8".	
TILED KITCHEN — TILED BATHROOM	SEPARATE W.C. — GARAGE SPACE.	

Equipment Includes:

ENCLOSED PANELLED BATH, MODERN LAV. BASIN, SHAVING CABINET, TOWEL RAIL, ETC.
PATENT CABINET DRESSER, GAS COPPER, INDEPENDENT BOILER, ETC.
TILED FIREPLACE SURROUNDS, ELECTRIC PANEL FIRE IN SECOND BEDROOM
ELECTRIC POINTS, ELECTRIC LIGHT FITTINGS, LAMPS AND SHADES SUPPLIED AND FIXED.
ALL SERVICE CHARGES FOR METERS PAID.

For further details or free car to view, write or 'phone:

DAVIS ESTATES L^TD

BUILDERS OF HOMES

ESTATE OFFICE ON SITE:
DOMONIC DRIVE,
SIDCUP ROAD,
NEW ELTHAM, S.E.9.
Tel.: ELTHAM 2286.

THE DAVIS SHOWHOUSE,
Adj. CHARING CROSS Stn.
25, VILLIERS STREET, W.C.2.
Tel.: TEMPLE BAR 7115/6.

N.B.—These particulars are intended to give a fair description, but do not constitute an offer or contract.

A 1935 POSTER for new houses at New Eltham.

BUCK'S TRANSPORT was started as an adjunct to the garage business in Footscray Road and many people remember this firm's removal work.

UNTIL NATIONALIZATION under the Act of 1947, Woolwich Borough Council was responsible for the electricity supply to all properties in the borough, and boxes with the council crests could be seen at the roadside, with some sporting street lamps. This surviving box stands in Eltham Palace Road.

PRE-FABS were erected on sites of bombed housing, public parks and other vacant spots after the Second World War to help ease the housing shortage. These units were at Horn Park Close.

BUILDING WORK STARTED ON THE COLDHARBOUR ESTATE in February 1947 and the first house, shown here at No. 2 Wynford Way, was officially opened by Minister of Health the Rt Hon. Aneurin Bevan MP on 12 July 1947.

COLDHARBOUR FARMHOUSE, among the new post-war houses at William Barefoot Drive and Spekehill, just before its demolition.

WESTHORNE BUNGALOWS were erected in the 1960s at the junction of Westhorne Avenue and Briset Road as a stop-gap measure to ease the housing shortage. This location alongside the railway was the cleared site of the Eltham Health Centre which was demolished by enemy action in the Second World War. This scene has greatly altered since the Rochester Way Relief Road has opened.

A 1950S AERIAL VIEW OF MOTTINGHAM VILLAGE before Porcupine Close and the nearby shops were built on the field at the junction of Court Road and Mottingham Road.

Shops and Services

AT THE JUNCTION OF WESTMONT ROAD AND GREENVALE ROAD were two small shop units one of which is shown here. The combined premises were later used as a Pricerite food shop but are now an office for the Woolwich Labour Party.

THE HIGH-NUMBERED SHOPS here in the High Street were originally known as The Broadway, and were developed as part of the Corbett Estate. The majestic structure with a spire was named the Monument by surveyor Thomas Chester Haworth who took Eltham off the cesspit drainage system. Some local people referred to it as the 'Monument to General Stink'!

SHOP ASSISTANT MR W.L. TESTER is seen at Mr W.A. Tooke's jeweller and watchmaker shop at No. 13 The Broadway, which is now the Eltham High Street Post Office and trades as C.H. Miles (Eltham) Ltd. Mr Tester later had his own shop at No. 71 Sidcup High Street.

THE FIRM OF J.B. FYSON had a bakery at their High Street premises (now the site of Boots). In 1928 production was moved to larger premises at a former drill hall near Southend Crescent. The smell of freshly-baked bread was familiar until 1970 when the bakery closed. The Whitewood removal firm now use the site.

A DECORATED HORSE-DRAWN FYSONS BREAD VAN ready for an Eltham parade of unknown date.

THE ELTHAM BRANCH OF THE 'NO RETREAT LODGE' look ready for an outing as they gather opposite The Rising Sun. The hardware shop of George Mence Smith can be seen plus the former Congregational church of 1839 which was replaced in 1930 by the Arcade and adjacent shops.

MR W. METCALFE'S FORGE IN THE HIGH STREET stood where the Woolworth store is today. Due to an impending civic development by Woolwich Borough Council Metcalfe's business moved to Pound Place in 1905 where it remained until 1987. On removal to new premises at Passey Place the old property was demolished in connection with the Sainsbury's development. Now trading as J. Metcalfe and specializing in lawn-mower repairs this family business is the longest established firm in Eltham.

FROM THE COBBLES AT THE JUNCTION OF ARCHERY ROAD AND THE HIGH STREET this 1929 picture shows the Roman Catholic church of St Mary's (1890) and adjacent buildings. The recent Sainsbury's development involved the demolition of this church and the naming of the new shopping parade as St Mary's Place.

HINDS STORE was opened in 1934 as a two-storey shop by Mr C.P. Hinds, chairman of the parent company at Blackheath. In 1936 extra floors were added which were served by a lift which is still in operation. Since a recent facelift to the frontage the store trades as Allders.

HINDS ROOF GARDEN formed part of the 1936 extension and was Eltham's popular spot for 'high' tea.

MR W. LAY STANDS WITH HIS WIFE and Miss D. Letchford in front of the Eltham Fruit Stores which he managed for the owner Mr Alf Elms. The shop stands near The Castle and is now used by a travel agent.

MR A.E. SIMPSON OWNED FURNITURE SHOPS AT THE BROADWAY but had once been a woodwork teacher at the Gordon School. His main store was opened in the High Street (now occupied by Currys) in 1922 as a two-storey showroom. Although bought out by Wheatlands during the Second World War the Simpson name was retained. The vans had a distinctive style which had no connection with Eltham but was adopted from a design used by another company.

THE THREE SHOPS SHOWN HERE and the British Road Services Eltham Parcels Depot were bought by Marks and Spencer for their present store which opened in 1975, while their previous accommodation was taken by Debenhams. The depot had been in use since the horse-drawn cart era, as witnessed by the cobbles where Mr A. Bassett is standing (opposite) prior to the yard's closure and transfer to Dartford.

MR BASSETT had worked at this depot for twenty-five years when it closed in April 1974.

THIS WAS THE FIRST ELTHAM CAVE AUSTIN GROCERY SHOP. A new store was built in the front garden of the adjacent Passey House and this shop was retained by Cave Austin as an off-licence. The High Street was renumbered in the mid 1930s and this property is now No. 106 and used by Cavendish Newsagents.

THE ELTHAM POST OFFICE as originally built at Passey Place in 1912. An extension completed the building in 1935 with a monogram to King George V featured above the main door. The removal of the Post Office and Sorting Office to new premises at Court Yard was completed in 1972.

MR G.J. BENJAFIELD ran this High Street shop by Passey Place from 1908–33. Former employee Mr H. Payn took over the business which his son Maurice Payn managed from 1964 until closure in 1977. The store specialized in men's clothing and also supplied uniforms for the scouts and guides.

ONE WONDERS WHAT SORT OF DELIVERIES WERE MADE from the Benjafield Outfitters on this bicycle. The shop stood at the corner of Passey Place and the High Street, and is seen on the previous page.

THIS 1930s VIEW OF THE HIGH STREET is readily recognizable today, although the Congregational church to the left has been replaced by the building now used by McDonalds.

THE EXPRESS DAIRY opened the first Eltham supermarket from these premises in 1952 and had a milk-bottling plant next to their depot in Court Yard where the Post Office buildings now stand. This view of 1964 shows Martins Bank, a milk machine outside the Express, the wartime porch outside The Greyhound and British-made vehicles at the traffic lights.

GRUMMITT'S STORES, COURT YARD, was once a family run hardware store, and two brothers are recorded on the Eltham War Memorial. It is now a Spastic Society charity shop and was previously used by Fads before they transferred to Grove Market Place in the former Pricerite supermarket.

MISS STAMPE was once the postmistress at the Eltham Post Office which operated until 1912 from a shop in Court Yard by a cul-de-sac called The Grove. It was last used as a sweet shop by the Beeson family and demolished as part of the Grove Market Place development which opened in 1967.

MEMBERS OF THE TUTT FAMILY at their first Eltham fresh-fish shop in Well Hall Road which is now Normans Music Shop. The business was transferred to the indoor market at Elm Terrace and then to the Arcade. A move was made to Pound Place where after many years trading they sold out to Joels in 1967.

THE FAMILY FIRM OF OUTTRIM were well-known carriers and their coal delivery vehicle is seen here on the Progress Estate.

THE RACS STORE at Well Hall was opened in 1906 for the residents of the new Corbett Estate. It included grocery, butchery and hardware departments and was replaced in 1964 by a new supermarket with flats above the store.

PEARKS GROCERY AND PROVISION STORES were a familiar sight on the smaller shopping parades like this one at No. 558 Westhorne Avenue. Other shops were at No. 69 Well Hall Road, No. 7 Newmarket Green and No. 731 Sidcup Road.

WESTMOUNT ROAD in the 1950s. Note the United Dairies milk float near their dairy shop.

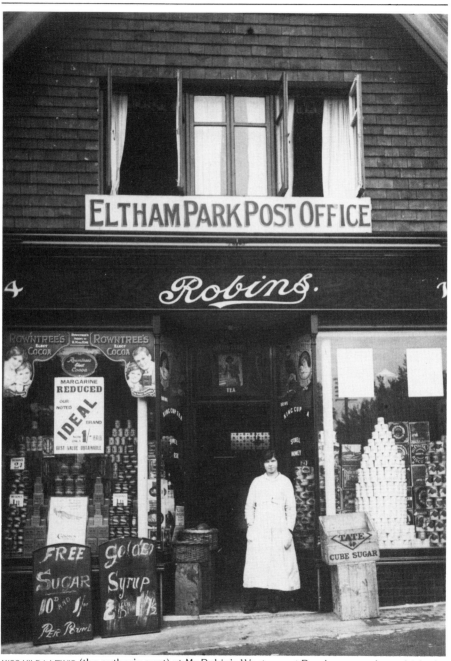

MISS HILDA LEWIS (the author's aunt) at Mr Robin's Westmount Road grocery shop which also included the Post Office in 1919. The sugar was not 'free' but 'free off ration'. The shop provides the same services today.

HAWES GREENGROCERY SHOP traded in Mottingham village until 1966. Horses for the local delivery service were kept behind the shop and are shown here.

A PROGRAMME OF EXPANSION through acquisition of small dairies brought the Express Dairy to Mottingham where they replaced an older dairy building with this depot for milk distribution. It sustained damage when the garage across the road received a direct hit in the Second World War and was rebuilt as seen here. It has now been converted into a car showroom.

THE UNITED DAIRIES MILK DISTRIBUTION DEPOT in Green Lane was opened by Sir Kingsley Wood MP in 1931. It has been replaced by the Dufton Business Park except for one building which is in office use.

A HORSE-DRAWN MILK CART at the Green Lane depot. Note the horse's tail has been docked, a recognized practice at this time. War damage to windows and glass panels can also be seen.

THE ORIGINAL BARTLETT'S STORES closed in 1973, having been at Footscray Road for almost eighty years. The Post Office was once housed here when the shops were known as Nos 6 and 7 The Parade. The three shops shown here have the original Victorian shopfronts.

THE MANAGER MR E. WICKHAM in the men's department at Bartlett's Stores in 1973.

MR S.F. HENLEY AND FAMILY outside his shop at No. 4 The Parade. The business is still run from this shop (now No. 393 Footscray Road), but with a modern shopfront.

MR ARTHUR 'RIDGE' WILLIAMS started his butchery business at this shop in 1939 after having worked for other local butchers. He is pictured here in 1961 with a representative from the Australian Meat Board after gaining first prize in a Smithfield competition. The business is now run by his son Bernard Williams.

THE FIRST RACS STORE at New Eltham attracted a large crowd when it was opened on 20 July 1921 by Mr J. Sheppard. It stood between the present store and the station-master's house on the left.

CORNER STYLE GROCERY SHOPS are rare these days in Eltham. This picture of the Service Stores at Green Lane was taken in 1968. The shop now trades as The Storage Equipment Centre.

ORIGINALLY ELM TERRACE had houses on both sides of this short road but only three survive and they have been turned into shops at pavement level. Hardcastles and the Elm Café are shown here in 1964. The building with the two arches started life as an indoor market in 1931 but only lasted a few years and is now used as a sports centre.

LOCAL CARRIER JOHN PEGG & SON operated for many years from New Eltham but has now ceased trading.

COAL DELIVERY IN SOUTHWOOD ROAD.

ELTHAM WAS SERVED BY THE LEE GREEN TELEPHONE EXCHANGE when this picture of Mr W. Outtrim's steam lorry was taken.

THIS DELIVERY VEHICLE AND HORSE were kept in the stable to the rear of The Man of Kent when Mr M.H. Choppin was the licensee.

SECTION FIVE

Transport

THE ELTHAM TO BLACKHEATH HORSE BUS was operated by Thomas Tillings between Blackheath and Eltham and stands here at The Broadway before its last journey in 1908.

THIS SOLID-TYRED B TYPE NO. 21 BUS from Palmers Green Garage stops for the camera at Eltham Green, probably during the First World War as there is a lady conductor. The driver had a draughty job with no windscreen protection, and the ladies on top must have had strong pins to hold down their hats.

THE NO. 21 BUS IS ELTHAM'S OLDEST BUS ROUTE, being first seen in 1914 when it ran between Crouch End and Sidcup. This external-staired LT type bus is seen outside Cave Austin grocery shop in the High Street on a short working to Well Hall station in 1948.

THESE BUSES WITH DOMED ROOFS were specially designed for operation through Rotherhithe and Blackwall tunnels and were known as Tunnel STLs. The No. 108a terminated at Cobbett Road by St Barnabas Church from 1944 and was extended to Southend Crescent in 1951. This driver is negotiating the Well Hall roundabout.

THE BUS STAND AT SOUTHEND CRESCENT during the Second World War when part of the bus mudguards were painted white. The brick wall belongs to the garden of Conduit Lodge.

BUS 182 PARTLY REPLACED TRAM ROUTE 46 in July 1952 when tram operation was abandoned in London. RT type buses are shown here at Well Hall bus station in Sherard Road.

UNTIL STATION ROAD WAS LOWERED BY SIDCUP STATION in 1958 the 228 route between Eltham and Chislehurst was restricted to single-decker buses. This side-engined Q type bus from Sidcup Garage awaits passengers at the High Street in 1949 as the billboard men advertise a television demonstration.

GREEN LINE route 703 passes Eltham Green on its way to Wrotham.

FOUR NEW MINI-BUS ROUTES were started in London in 1972 using roads which were not suitable for larger vehicles. One of these routes was the B1 which ran between Bromley and Eltham. On the short working between Bromley and New Eltham the bus terminated here at Reventlow Road.

WELL HALL STATION opened in 1895 when the Bexleyheath line between Blackheath and Dartford (approx.) was inaugurated. This picture of 1969 shows the original 'Down-side' shelter. The shelter has been saved for preservation by a railway group, as the station was demolished in 1985 due to the opening of the adjacent Eltham Station. A railway bridge over the new A2 highway (Rochester Way Relief Road) covers the old station site.

ELTHAM PARK STATION was known as Shooters Hill station when it opened in 1908 with the main office buildings at road level. With the introduction of electric trains in 1926 the ticket office was relocated at platform level and this building was converted into the Station Parade shops with the former ticket office becoming the chemist's shop. The shops remain but the station was demolished in 1985.

A NOSTALGIC VIEW taken from the Glenesk Road bridge looking to Eltham Park station with a Kent Coast excursion passing the large brick electrical sub-station in 1950. During the week the coaches were kept at a siding by Blackheath station.

FARMER BROWN'S BRIDGE was built in 1866 for cows to graze in the fields at either side of the railway. As it had long been out of use it was officially blown up by British Rail in 1971.

'NEW ELTHAM FOR POPE STREET' is stated on the station sign as a steam engine engages the 'Down' platform while a haycart at Station Approach passes the main station building.

A DIESEL-HAULED TRAIN was travelling greatly in excess of a 20 m.p.h. speed limit as it hit the sharp curve outside Well Hall station. It left the track and piled up on part of the former goods yard. This happened on 11 June 1972 and six passengers on this railwaymen's excursion returning from the Kent coast died as a result of the crash. The picture shows some of the wreckage.

THE SHOPS AT WELL HALL PARADE were built to serve the residents of the new Corbett Estate. For a wider shopping choice they could take the tram to Woolwich to sample the delights of Cuffs and Garretts stores, or search for bargains at Woolwich Market.

THE TERMINUS FOR THE WOOLWICH TRAMS by St John's church promoted the construction in 1912 of the first public toilets at Well Hall Road. In 1922 a new block was opened for men while the original block was converted for female use; a tram shelter (now closed) stands between the two blocks.

A BUSY TRAFFIC JUNCTION at the High Street crossroads. The No. 44 tram will scrape its wheels on the curved rails on its way down the hill to Middle Park Avenue and The Yorkshire Grey. Burton's store replaced the Congregational church which was relocated in Court Road and is now known as the United Reform church. McDonalds bought the former Burton's shop and have operated here since 1979. The downstairs seating area incorporates the original church basement.

A GOOD LOADING FOR THIS WOOLWICH TRAM is guaranteed by the crowds in Well Hall Road opposite the police station. Churchyard Cottages (p. 149) once stood here. Some of the last London trams ran on Eltham routes in July 1952.

THE TRAM OPERATOR CHANGES THE POINTS at the Well Hall roundabout to take route 72 along Westhorne Avenue. A police telephone box can be seen in front of some Progress Estate houses.

THE RAILWAY BRIDGE AT WESTHORNE AVENUE was completed in 1932 and enabled tram route 72 to use this road. The scene has been transformed by the works that were necessary to accommodate the Rochester Way Relief Road.

TRAM ROUTE 44 RAN BETWEEN WOOLWICH AND MIDDLE PARK AVENUE via 'Eltham Church' and changed tracks at the points here by Eltham Green Road, where the conductor waits to re-fix the pole for the return journey to Woolwich.

AN OVERTURNED LORRY BY ST JOHN'S CHURCH at Well Hall Road in 1924 attracts much attention. The tram has a twin trolley pole which was unique to the Eltham–Woolwich route as the Astronomer Royal at Greenwich thought that without an extra return the electricity would affect the delicate instruments at the Observatory.

THESE TWO PICTURES SHOW THE LONDON TO RAMSGATE MAIL CONVOY which has stopped at Avery Hill possibly due to a vehicle breakdown. Note the fuel cans strapped to the mail van above the driver's cab in the lower picture.

A DECORATED CART of the London Parcels Delivery Company poses in Court Yard for a local parade.

HORACE CLIFF started his motor coach business at Well Hall in 1921. His vehicles were garaged on land which is now part of Well Hall Pleasaunce.

AFTER REMOVAL FROM WELL HALL, Cliff's kept their coaches here at Footscray Road from 1936 to 1978. This site has been redeveloped for use by the building firm Bryen Langley.

THE DRIVER OF A GRUNDON'S COACH is ready to take a party from Novar Hall, Novar Road on an outing. The firm kept their coaches in a nearby yard in Avery Hill Road which is now used for parking British Telecom vehicles.

THE LANGTON FAMILY of No. 53 Grenvale Road prepare to take to the road in this roomy car. Mr E.S. Langton was a photographer who produced local postcards which he sold from a board in his front garden. His card of the National Reserve is shown on p. 133.

A PAPERBOY waits at the junction of Court Road and Sidcup Road. The Royal Hotel was rebuilt in 1934 to the plans of architect Alfred Blomfield who also designed Eltham Park station. The original public house stood nearer to Mottingham station.

SIDCUP ROAD showing the ribbon housing development alongside this major trunk route to Kent with Leysdown Road to the right. Later main road housing was only permitted behind a service road, as can be seen on the Sidcup Road between West Park and King John's Walk.

MOTORISTS QUEUING FOR PETROL AT CLIFTONS GARAGE on the Sidcup Road in September 1939.

THE SIDCUP ROAD GARAGE was taken over by Cliffords of Sidcup in 1954 having been in the ownership of Halse & Co. since the mid-1920s. The redeveloped site is now operated by Q8.

ALTHOUGH THESE PREMISES IN FOOTSCRAY ROAD ARE TRADING AS GRUNDON'S GARAGE they were known for many years as Buck's Garage. This site near Green Lane has been redeveloped for petrol sales but the old farm building, which is Grade II listed, can still be seen.

A 1930s VIEW OF HITCHES GARAGE and the car showrooms. The petrol pumps stand in front of the house which was the first home of the Eltham and Mottingham Cottage Hospital in 1880.

FOR MANY YEARS MR RUSHOLM BROWN RAN THE CENTRAL GARAGE which occupied the site of the gardens of Sherard House and Merlewood House. Sherard House was demolished to make way for the Westminster Bank, while Merlewood House was replaced by single-storey shops in the High Street. A telephone exchange has been built on the garage site and named Merlewood House. The Central petrol pump is shown in 1970 when the fuel was 6s. 1d. a gallon.

GLENLEA GARAGE was run for many years by Mr J. Bowers at the corner of Glenlea Road and Westmount Road. The picture opposite shows a parade of new Ford cars with sequenced number plates while this view includes the rear of the shops in Westmount Road. All of these buildings were demolished for the construction of the Rochester Way Relief Road and the garage site is now covered with a landscaped area and footpath.

MR E. BECKETT brought his motor cycle business to Court Yard in 1947 which was started with his father in 1920 from a hut near Well Hall station. A service depot was later added here at Blunts Road which was used until the land was required for the Fifteenpenny Fields Almshouses. New premises were taken behind Mellins in the High Street where motor scooters were also repaired. Three shops were eventually used at Court Yard but for car sales. The business has now transferred to Hatherley Road, Sidcup, under the direction of Mr Beckett's two sons.

PRE-SECOND WORLD WAR POLICE VEHICLES in the yard of the old police station at the corner of Footscray Road and the High Street. The station operated from 1865 until 1939 when the new premises opened in Well Hall Road to the design of Roger Pinckney.

THE ODDLY NAMED MOTTINGHAM AMBULANCE STATION by The Yorkshire Grey opened in 1955, some distance from Mottingham.

A FIRE necessitated the demolition of George's women's wear shop in 1961. The store was to the same external design as Mellins next door, but had been enlarged. The shop built on this site is now occupied by W.H. Smith.

THE CONTRIBUTION OF VOLUNTEERS, particularly women, to local services during the Second World War is shown in these two pictures. One of the duties of the Women's Voluntary Service (WVS) was to cook meals for army personnel at Sutcliffe Park where this group picture was taken. The lower picture shows the two Eltham detachments of the British Red Cross Society whose respective commandants were Miss K. McKay and Miss Adams. They served in various ways: at first-aid posts, public shelters, as hospital nurses and with ambulance crews. They are shown in the grounds of Tilt Yard House which was then owned by Miss Adams.

Education and Leisure

EALDHAM SQUARE SCHOOL SECOND XI, 1932/3 football team with Mr Jackson.

MAYPOLE DANCERS in the garden of Penshurst School at No. 94 Southwood Road. The school was founded by Miss Daisy Short and her sister Violet in 1914 and closed in 1969.

EMPIRE DAY WAS A GREAT PATRIOTIC OCCASION as shown at the Gordon School in 1912. The school is named after the famous soldier General Charles Gordon who was born at Woolwich in 1833.

THE NATIONAL INFANTS SCHOOL at Back Lane (now Philipot Path) opened in 1852 and a group of children from the 1920s are shown here with their headmistress, Miss A. Roberts, who is wearing glasses. As the Eltham Church of England Infants School it moved to new buildings at Roper Street in 1933.

THE ELTHAM NATIONAL SCHOOL AT ROPER STREET was built in 1868 and is still used for educating children, although now known as Eltham Church of England School. In 1932 these Empire Day maypole dancers were providing entertainment where the infant building now stands.

A CLASS OF GIRLS at Deansfield Road School in 1928.

CROWN WOODS SCHOOL opened as a mixed comprehensive school in 1958. Since this picture was taken a boarding lodge has been added as have extra classrooms to cope with the raising of the school-leaving age.

THE CORONATION OF THE MAY QUEEN at Montbelle School in 1935, when the school was housed in the wooden buildings which were opened a couple of years earlier. Extra classrooms and other facilities were officially opened by (Sir) Peter Scott in 1955.

FOLLOWING THE PUBLICATION of Robert Baden-Powell's book *Scouting for Boys*, the Scout Movement started in 1907. Local lads soon took an interest and their district was called Royal Eltham, in deference to the historic associations with Eltham Palace. Early members of the 1st Royal Eltham Troop are shown here.

Royal Eltham Association of Wolf Cubs, Scouts & Rovers

President - - - EVERARD HESKETH, Esq.
District Commissioner - C. A. FEATHERSTONE, Esq.

PROGRAMME OF THE

Official Opening

of the

ASSOCIATION
CAMPING GROUND

off Bexley Road, Eltham.

By Deputy Camp Chief W. J. GENESE

at 4 p.m. on

Saturday, May 30th, 1931

to be followed by the Inter-Troop
CINEMA CUP COMPETITION FOR SCOUTCRAFT
and
SCOUT and WOLF CUB DISPLAYS.

Music by the Band of the 1st New Cross Troop B.P. Scouts.
BANDMASTER - MR. HIRRILD

Teas, Refreshments and Sideshows at popular price.

PROGRAMME   TWOPENCE

THE CINEMA CUP referred to on this programme was presented by the directors of the Palace Cinema, Eltham, in 1926 and has been competed for by scout troops ever since. The author led the winning patrol in 1955.

A LARGE CROWD has gathered to see a range of scouting activities on the opening of the Association Camping Ground on 30 May 1931. Avery Hill Estate now covers this open land.

A WORKING PARTY OF SCOUTS from the 4th Royal Eltham Troop at the Avery Hill Camping Ground. Third from the right is Pat Bashford who later settled in Rhodesia as a farmer. He became leader of the Centre Party before the country became independent as Zimbabwe.

THE ST GEORGE'S DAY SERVICE for local scouts and cubs was held at Eltham Park Methodist Church in 1955. The 12th Royal Eltham Sea Scouts are parading here at Westmount Road.

GIRL GUIDES FROM ST BARNABAS' CHURCH doing a 'good deed' at the Eltham War Memorial.

CHURCH PARADE TIME for some girl guides from St Barnabas' church as they are pictured at Sandby Green.

FAMOUS GOLFERS HARRY VARDON AND JAMES BRAID are featured on this Ogden's cigarette card at Eltham; probably playing at the Eltham Golf Club Course (now Royal Blackheath).

WELL HALL PLEASAUNCE was opened to the public in 1933 and the newly created bowling green and putting green can be seen. The bowling pavilion had a thatched roof.

THE NEW ELTHAM BOWLS CLUB on their ground behind The Beehive. Landlord Bob Choppin took a keen interest in the club which was founded by his father Mr Mace Choppin. After Courage took over the public house from Beasleys they sold the land for housing.

A FAIR of the 1930s at the Pippenhall open space on the Bexley Road was opened by Sir Kingsley Wood MP and included a wall of death ride.

gt. aunt Pheobe Basker

Mr Elizabeth Basker (Una's Mum)

THE MUNITION WORKERS' HOSTELS (p. 56) were removed in the early 1920s and permanent housing was built at Archery Road and Dobell Road. This piece of land was leased to the Royal Eltham Miniature Golf Course Co. Ltd but was not a financial success. The houses at Elstow Close were subsequently built here by Alfred Wright and the former clubhouse (below) was converted into a bungalow.

golfer Basker Brothers una

Grand Basker Una's Grandpa

WOOLWICH BOROUGH COUNCIL provided this mobile library for locations like Avery Hill and Coldharbour which were some distance from a public library. The vehicle is shown here in 1957 at Gregory Crescent off Middle Park Avenue.

ELTHAM CINEMA THEATRE opened in 1913 near the junction of the High Street and Westmount Road. Maurice Crisp, on the left of the group, was the projectionist, while his sister Leila played the piano to accompany the silent films. The main building was demolished in 1968 having long been out of use as a cinema, though an adjoining rear building survives. This is now used as offices by Honour Installations. The Eltham Mini Town Hall, built in 1973, stands on an adjacent site.

THE PALACE CINEMA THEATRE was opened in 1922, being advertised as the latest in cinema luxury. 'Talkies' came in 1930, when *Innocents of Paris* starring Maurice Chevalier was screened. In the 1950s the distinctive dome was removed from the top of the building and closure of the cinema came in 1972. The shopping parade at the junction of the High Street and Passey Place now stands at this site.

A COACH PARTY FROM THE KINGS ARMS seem all prepared for their outing as they pose for the camera.

People and Events

A 1953 CORONATION PARTY at St Luke's Hall, Westmount Road. The fancy dress contestants probably came from Dumbreck Road.

DURING THE FIRST WORLD WAR Southwood House (Roper Hall) at Avery Hill College was taken over by the Red Cross Society as a convalescent home for injured servicemen.

VETERANS OF PREVIOUS CAMPAIGNS on parade at the Gordon School as members of the No. 9 Company (Eltham) National Reserve. Perhaps this is an earlier version of the Home Guard.

LARGE CROWDS attended the unveiling of the Eltham War Memorial at St John's church by Field Marshal Sir Wm Robertson in 1924. A wreath laying ceremony is held here every year on Remembrance Sunday.

THE CASTELLATED IVY-CLAD FRONTAGE OF THIS BUILDING belies its use as a factory by Walter Grafton whose firm became famous for the manufacture of typewriter spools. The segregated workforce in this picture appear to be part of a newspaper promotion by the *Daily Graphic*. The B&Q store has been built on this site and opened in 1988.

AN INTERIOR VIEW of Grafton's factory showing the ladies at work.

A WEDDING GROUP in the garden of one of the hutments at Venus Road in the 1920s.

THE GREEN AT RANCLIFFE GARDENS was the setting for this large coronation party in 1937.

THIS MEMORIAL AT ST JOHN'S CHURCHYARD is to aborigine Yemmerrawanyea Kebbarah who died at Eltham while visiting this country in 1794. His companion Benelong returned to Australia and ended his days at a site which became known as Benelong Point, where the Sydney Opera House has now been built.

THOMAS CHESTER HAWORTH, the Eltham surveyor, established this family wayside tomb at Beaconsfield Road, Mottingham, with the first burial in 1875. Second World War damage robbed the tomb of its original dimensions and the family remains have been re-interred under stone plaques.

MR HENRY WHISTLER ran a building business with relation Mr Worge from a shop near The Greyhound, with later removal to Pound Place. His son Rex Whistler was born at No. 5 Park Place (now Passey Place) in 1905 and later received great acclaim as an artist. The family moved to Bryher at Court Road (now site of the United Reform Church) where Laurence was born in 1912. He is now a highly respected glass engraver and biographer of Rex.

THE BEAVER HOUSING SOCIETY owns houses in Keightley Drive, Oakley Drive and Beaverbank Road where this seat was erected to commemorate Colonel Roberts the founder of the society.

THIS BAROMETER of contributions to War Weapons Week stood near a boarded up Burton's shop, sometime during the Second World War.

THE SUCCESSFUL RIFLE SQUAD of the 21st County of London (Eltham) Home Guard Battalion, display their trophies at Southend Hall. General Brownrigg is seated on the middle chair and Mr H. Trodd stands on the extreme left.

A VICTORY PARADE led by the Royal Artillery Band passes along the High Street by Westmount Road after the Second World War.

A VICTORY IN EUROPE (VE) party at Castleton Road, Mottingham.

THE WOOLWICH CORONATION PROCESSION has passed St Luke's church in Westmount Road after its journey from Woolwich on 4 June 1953.

EVENING CROWDS WAIT FOR THE WOOLWICH CORONATION PROCESSION at the Well Hall round-about. A decorative centrepiece was erected by the Woolwich Borough Council.

EDITH NESBIT stands at the centre of the back row with a family group in her Eltham home. Well Hall became the setting for some of her books including *The Red House* and *The Wouldbegoods*.

Opposite:

RICHARD JEFFERIES came to live with his family at No. 14 Victoria Road in 1884. His reputation as a writer on nature and country matters continued, but his health deteriorated and he moved to Crowborough. His memorial at Worthing Cemetery is inscribed: *Richard Jefferies, Prose Poet of England's Fields and Woodlands*

THIS BLUE PLAQUE was unveiled by Cllr Jim Gillman, Mayor of Greenwich, at Richard Jefferies' former Eltham home, now known as No. 59 Footscray Road, in 1986.

Faithfully yours
Richard Jefferies

CHARLES STEWART PARNELL AT WONERSH LODGE.

THE ROMANCE between Katharine O'Shea and Charles Stewart Parnell was the subject of a 1991 BBC TV drama called *Parnell and the Englishwoman*. Captain O'Shea and his wife Katharine moved to North Park in 1876 so that she could visit her aunt Mrs Ben Wood who lived nearby at Eltham Lodge. After the O'Sheas divorced Katharine married Parnell but he died a few months later in 1891.

WONERSH LODGE, THE HOME OF THE O'SHEAS, was later renamed Dunclutha; as No. 51 North Park it was demolished in 1964 with other large Victorian houses and replaced by the flats of Woodington Close.

KATHARINE O'SHEA was also known as 'Kitty' O'Shea.

BEARDED DR W.G. GRACE with fellow members of the Eltham Cricket Club which he joined when he came to live at Mottingham in 1909.

MR S. CHIESMAN UNVEILS THE BLUE PLAQUE to Dr W.G. Grace in 1966 at Fairmount, Mottingham Lane, where the famous cricketer lived from 1909 until his death in 1915.

LABOUR POLITICIAN HERBERT MORRISON lived at No. 55 Archery Road from 1929 to 1960. This blue plaque was unveiled by Greater London Council leader Sir Reg Goodwin in 1972. A policeman could often be seen outside the house when Herbert Morrison held high governmental office. The 'Morrison' indoor air-raid shelter was named after him during his period as Home Secretary in the Second World War. From 1923 to 1929, he lived in Well Hall Road, and between 1960 and 1965 in Colepits Wood Road.

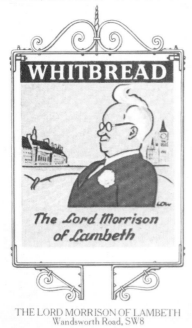

THE LORD MORRISON OF LAMBETH
Wandsworth Road, SW8

HERBERT MORRISON was created a life peer in 1959 and took the title of Lord Morrison of Lambeth. A public house was named after him in Wandsworth Road SW8 and he had the pleasure of opening it in 1962.

CHURCHYARD COTTAGES by St John's church in what is now Well Hall Road. Mr George Croydon Marks was born here in 1858.

MR MARKS entered the Royal Arsenal School in Woolwich and later became a successful engineer, being particularly associated with the building of cliff railways at Lynton and Lynmouth, Saltburn and Bridgnorth. He became MP for Launceston in 1906 and was knighted in 1911. On elevation to the peerage in 1929 he took the title Baron Marks of Woolwich, and died at his Bournemouth home in 1938.

MR S. COURTAULD OF ELTHAM PALACE was a patron of Eltham scouting, and he is seen here seated with his wife at a reception for scouts from Barbados in 1937. They were in England after attending a Jamboree in Holland and camped in the grounds of Eltham Palace.

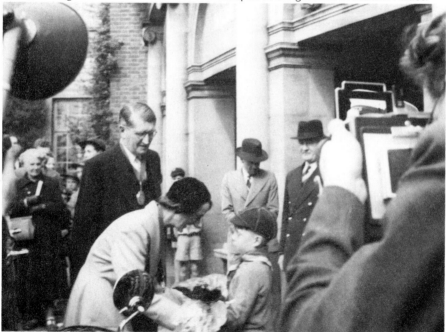

THE MAYOR AND MAYORESS OF WOOLWICH, Councillor J.W. and Mrs Andrews, are greeted by a young member of the 12th Royal Eltham Scout Group at their fête in the grounds of Eltham Palace in 1954. The recent housing development near Holy Trinity church has been named Andrews Place to commemorate this former mayor.

THE 12TH ROYAL ELTHAM SCOUT GROUP take over the grounds of Eltham Palace for their fête. Due to security problems events of this nature are no longer possible for the general public.

THE QUEEN IN COURT YARD after attending the 50th anniversary celebrations of the Royal Army Education Corps at Eltham Palace in 1972.

HER MAJESTY QUEEN ELIZABETH THE QUEEN MOTHER at The Mound in 1957 on the occasion of the official completion of the Coldharbour Estate.

A GROUP OF MEMBERS OF THE ELTHAM CONSERVATIVE CLUB pictured in front of the present premises in the High Street. Fourth from the left on the front row is Sir Kingsley Wood MP.

Eltham's Members of Parliament

From 1832 to 1885 Eltham was part of the Western Division of Kent. From 1885 to 1918 it was part of Woolwich and the longest serving MP was Will Crooks. Due to an expanding population Woolwich was split into two constituencies and Eltham became part of West Woolwich from 1918 to 1983. The appropriate geographical name for most of the constituency 'Eltham' was effected in 1983.

MPs for Woolwich West

Sir H. Kingsley-Wood	(Con.)	1918–43
Major Francis Beech	(Con.)	1943–5
Henry Berry	(Lab.)	1945–50
Sir William Steward	(Con.)	1950–9
Colin Turner	(Con.)	1959–64
William Hamling	(Lab.)	1964–75
Peter Bottomley	(Con.)	1975–83

MP for Eltham since 1983
Peter Bottomley

ELTHAM PARK (SOUTH) STILL HAD A RURAL ASPECT when designated for public use in 1902. The early plans for the Corbett Estate included housing here, but the local authorities stepped in and bought the land for recreational use.

THESE COTTAGES STOOD NEAR THE PRINCE OF WALES in Mottingham Road and were demolished in 1938.

THE ELTHAM BYPASS (now known as the Sidcup Road) was opened in May 1923 by the Parliamentary Secretary of the Ministry of Transport, Colonel Wilfrid W. Ashley MP (father of Lady Mountbatten) who declared the road open 'for the subjects of the King for ever.'

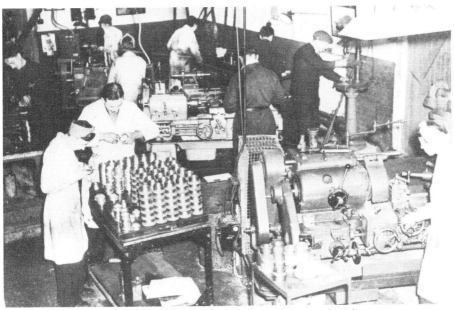

CAR REPAIRS GAVE WAY TO WAR WORK at Clifton's Garage when aircraft components were manufactured during the Second World War.

MR F. MINDE, MANAGER OF THE ODEON CINEMA (later Gaumont), Eltham Hill from 1945 to 1952, is pictured with Bob Hope who was born at No. 44 Craigton Road on 29 May 1903. The Eltham Little Theatre has been renamed as The Bob Hope Theatre and was visited by the great man himself in 1980 and 1982.

THE ANCIENT OFFICE OF PARISH BEADLE has been retained as a ceremonial role by St John's church. An Edwardian holder of the post is seen here.

RESIDENTS OF QUEENSCROFT ROAD prepare to celebrate the 1937 coronation with a party in the Church Mission Hall at Mayerne Road.

MR H. JONES OF SIBTHORPE ROAD, HORN PARK, received a certificate of merit from the London Gardens Society in the summer of 1951 for 'Creating a garden suitable for Her Majesty the Queen to visit.' The civic heads of Lewisham and Woolwich look on as the Queen congratulates Mr and Mrs Jones in a garden at Grove Park.

AS PART OF THE RECENT SAINSBURY'S DEVELOPMENT the building to the right in this Edwardian view has been restored for public use as the St Mary's Community and Resource Centre. In the 1850s it was the boyhood home of the future Lord Goschen and later occupation was for school purposes. The present use for a fine historical building is most welcome in Eltham.

ELTHAM'S ONLY TOWN SIGN was erected in the days of the Woolwich Borough Council and stands on the footpath by St John's church.

ACKNOWLEDGEMENTS

My thanks are hereby recorded to the people who have helped me with my researches into Eltham's history over many years and have loaned pictures for reproduction, particularly fellow members of The Eltham Society, members of my Eltham Past & Present evening class, Mr Gus White, the staff of the Greenwich Local History Library and local residents.

For this volume I have used pictures from my own collection which include contributions from:

Mrs D. Ajegbo ● Mrs H. Armstrong ● Mr W. Atterton ● Mrs S. Baker
Mr E. Beckett ● Mr J. Bowers ● Mr J. Bury ● Miss M. Cameron ● Mr C. Carter
Mrs F.Case ● Mr R. Clifford ● Mr F. Coldwell ● Mr G. Corp ● Mr E. Course
Mr E. Cowdry ● Mr M. Crisp ● Mr A. Cross ● Mrs A. Gibson ● Mr L. Hardwell
Mr W. Haynes ● Mr P. Heard ● Miss M. Henley ● Mr A. Jackson ● Mr H. Jones
Mr J. Kennett ● Mrs E. Kemble ● Mrs N. Lockett ● Mr F. McDermott (via
Mrs B. Fleming and Mrs P. Human) ● Mrs M. Minde ● Mr J. Morris
Mrs B. Palmer ● Mr D. Parker ● Mr M. Payn ● Mrs G. Perkins ● Mr G. Pugh
Miss M. Ray ● Mrs P. Sharman ● Mr N. Smidmore ● Mr and Mrs G. Smith
Mrs C. Thomas ● Mrs B. Thorpe ● Miss P. Webb ● Mr R. Weston
Mr G. White ● Mr B. Williams ● Mr J. Wiseman ● Mrs M. Wootton ● Mr G. Wroe
RACS ● *News Shopper*

My apologies for any omissions.